The Paper Jewelry Book

Jessica Wrobel

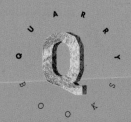

Rockport Publishers, Inc.
Gloucester, Massachusetts
Distributed by North Light Books
Cincinnati, Ohio

First published in the United States of America by
Quarry Books, an imprint of
Rockport Publishers, Inc.
33 Commercial Street
Gloucester, Massachusetts 01930
Telephone: (508) 282-9590
Fax: (508) 283-2742

Distributed to the book trade and art trade in the United States by
North Light Books, an imprint of
F & W Publications
1507 Dana Avenue
Cincinnati, Ohio 45207
Telephone: (800) 289-0963

Other Distribution by
Rockport Publishers, Inc.
Gloucester, Massachusetts 01930

ISBN 1-56496-350-0

10 9 8 7 6 5 4 3 2

Design: Lynn Pulsifer
Photography: Michael Lafferty

Printed in Hong Kong
by Midas Printing Limited.

739.27
W

# Contents

**4**

Introduction and Basic Supplies

Introduction and
Basic Supplies

Most of us use paper every day without giving it much thought. The purpose of this book is to introduce you to some jewelry making techniques and projects that will open the door to a whole new world of creative opportunities with paper.

Paper is a medium that is accessible to everyone. As you work on the projects in this book, you will find that all kinds of paper, from the contents of your recycling bin to expensive wrapping paper, can be transformed into beautiful jewelry. Before you begin working with paper, you should understand the basic nature of paper and cardboard, also known as chipboard. The fibers of each of these materials are formed in such a way that they line up and point in one direction, called the grain. You can use this characteristic to your advantage because the paper and board will bend, fold, and tear more easily if you make your folds and tears parallel to the grain.

Work will always progress more quickly and easily when you are working with the right tools. A ruler is essential for making accurate measurements, and straight lines and cuts. In most cases, a craft knife is the best paper-cutting tool, but sometimes you will need the versatility of scissors. Keep two different sizes of scissors handy. Use small scissors to cut out delicate decoupage pieces and larger, sturdier scissors to cut through heavier materials such as chipboard.

The glue that you use, and the tools that you use to apply it, will also affect how easy it is to complete the project. Polyvinyl acetate (PVA) is a very strong, flexible white glue that is easy to work with and dries quickly. It is available in many art supply stores and bookbinder supply shops. There are two tools you can use for applying glue, depending on the project. Use a squeeze bottle for narrow beads or dots of glue, but to cover larger areas, use a brush to apply the glue.

Lastly, a good pair of needle-nosed pliers is indispensable for holding onto the small jewelry findings that are necessary for turning a beautiful piece of paper craft into a personal accessory.

Jewelry findings are indispensable to the jewelry making process. Available in craft stores in either silver or gold color, they form, attach, or close jewelry pieces. The findings used to link together paper jewelry in this book are jump rings, small metal rings that can be opened to thread through a jewelry piece and then closed again to secure everything in place; and eye pins and head pins, short, straight pieces of wire with a stop at one end to prevent jewelry items such as paper beads from sliding off the end. An eye pin has a small circle of wire at the end so that it can be linked to other items, and the head pin is capped by a flat disk of metal like a sewing pin. Jewelry findings used in this book include the barrel clasp in the Flapper's Bead Necklace (page 14) which looks like a cylinder whose two halves screw into one another. The spring ring clasp that closes the Origami Fold Bracelet (page 66) resembles a jump ring with a small latch so that it can be opened and closed by hand. The Golden Braid Choker (page 62) clasp comes in two pieces that hook together with a latch and chain. Each of the two pieces has a decorative metal clamp that is pinched down over each end of the paper that makes up the necklace.

The paper beading, folding, and weaving techniques featured here are very simple and the results can look very professional, but be sure to take your time when laying out the projects to assure a beautiful piece of paper jewelry. Once you have learned a technique, experiment to discover variations in design. Most of all, enjoy the process and the inherent rewards of your creative undertakings.

Pointers

▶ **Keep a sharp point on your pencil to assure accurate measurements.**

▶ **If you cannot find $1/32$" (.75 mm) chipboard, substitute cardboard from cereal boxes.**

▶ **Use an indelible marker when adding details to a project—anything else will smear when you add the finish coat of polyurethane.**

▶ **Keep craft knives and scissors very sharp to make the neatest cuts.**

▶ **Shorten or lengthen necklace and bracelet patterns to fit your size and proportions. Adjust other patterns to suit your needs.**

*M*aking paper beads is a simple craft that can yield elegant results. Beads can be linked for necklaces and earrings, strung together to make chokers, bracelets, and hair ornaments, or used to decorate papier-mâché or woven paper jewelry.

Paper beads traditionally were created by winding a paper strip around a knitting needle or a nail. The length of a bead is determined by the measurement of the widest part of the paper strip, and the thickness by the length of the strip, the weight of the paper stock, and the size of the center hole.

A cotter pin can be substituted for the knitting needle or nail. The pin has two legs that act as a gripping device and make it easier to wind the bead with the appropriate tension. The gauge or thickness of the cotter pin will also determine the size of the bead's center hole. Hardware stores carry a wide assortment of cotter pins.

Paper Bead Jewelry

The paper you choose for your jewelry depends on the project and your taste. Marbled papers lend themselves beautifully to paper beads; so do paste paper, vellum, handmade paper, and wrapping paper. Even papers with rather mundane patterns can yield surprising results when wrapped into beads. Once you have made and decorated the beads, they can simply be strung together. You will need about thirty, $3/4$" (2 cm) beads to make a medium-length necklace, and ten or twelve for a single-strand bracelet.

To begin the design process, collect an assortment of papers that vary in pattern, color, and texture, and lay them out in front of you. Shuffle and reshuffle the papers until you find some pieces that work well together, then cut the paper into strips about 5" to 7" (13 cm to 18 cm) long. The shape of the paper strip will determine the shape of the bead: triangular pieces of paper make rounded beads; an isosceles triangle (two sides of equal length) makes an oval or spherical bead; an asymmetrical triangle makes a teardrop; a rectangular strip makes a cylindrical bead.

How to Make
Paper Beads

▸ Cut out paper strips with pinking shears or curved- and wavy-edge novelty scissors (available at most arts and crafts stores) to give beads an interesting texture.

▸ To make patterned beads, back a straight-edged strip with a strip of the same size cut with a pair of novelty scissors.

▸ Glue together two or more strips of different colors—make one strip slightly larger than the other—for a beautiful, multicolored spiral effect.

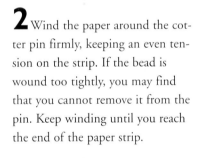

1 To start, slip one end of the paper strip (the widest end of the triangular pieces) under one leg of the cotter pin.

▸ To make beads with large center holes, try using a toothpick or a knitting needle instead of a cotter pin.

▸ If a bead is wound too tightly to remove from the cotter pin, gently twist the entire bead in the opposite direction from which it was wound. This should slightly unwind the bead and loosen it enough to slide from the pin.

2 Wind the paper around the cotter pin firmly, keeping an even tension on the strip. If the bead is wound too tightly, you may find that you cannot remove it from the pin. Keep winding until you reach the end of the paper strip.

▸ You may find thick papers difficult to roll up. The thinner the paper, the easier it is to handle. If you want a thicker paper bead, use a longer paper strip.

▸ To finish paper beads, use water-based polyurethane: it won't yellow and it dries within a few hours. A coat of polyvinyl acetate (PVA) glue is a good alternative to polyurethane but is not as durable.

3 Secure the end of the strip to the finished bead with a small dot of glue. Hold the end in place until the glue sets, then gently slide the bead off the cotter pin. Let dry for about an hour. When they are dry, slip two beads at a time back onto the cotter pin and use a small brush to apply PVA glue or polyurethane.

▸ You may want to leave beads uncoated, but be aware that any bead that touches the body is likely to discolor and pill as it absorbs oils from the skin.

Making the Jewelry

I learned about paper beads from my grandmother, who made them as a girl. After a long day of work, she and her sisters would gather in the kitchen to design and string beautiful paper bead curtains that would afford them a little privacy in their small living quarters. For them, it was both a social and creative gathering. They used remnants of wallpaper, cut into strips and rolled around a nail. A dot of white glue secured the bead, and several coats of varnish were applied as a finish before the beads were strung together. In this manner, they created colorful draperies one bead at a time.

Use nylon, silk, or cotton thread and a beading needle—or try stringing beads on silk cord, narrow ribbon, or fine-gauge wire. String multiple strands and twist them into a colorful rope, or make strands of tiny paper beads and braid them together for a woven effect. Add knots, spacer beads, or charms between paper beads for color or texture contrast.

The light weight of paper beads can make them hard to balance: if they are strung too tightly, the strand will buckle instead of hanging straight down; if they are strung too loosely, portions of the strand will show between beads or gravity will pull all the beads down toward the center. The gaps will be exposed on the strand behind the neck.

Also, if the center hole is not large enough for the strand and you push too hard, the bead will "telescope" out.

Beading Tips

For a *fancier* design, thread several strands through a single large bead, then separate them to work each strand individually, before bringing them back together through another single bead.

Bead *multiple* strands individually, bring together through a large bead, and separate again on the other side.

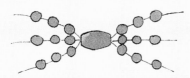

Join *beads* with eye pins or head pins for a glint of gold or silver between each bead.

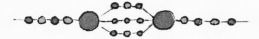

Curl *short* strands of beads in a spiral and glue to a pin or earring back.

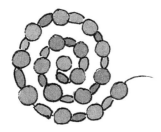

Triple Strand *Bracelet*

Sometimes there are treasures hiding in the back corner of a storage drawer, like this wonderful red paper threaded with delicate gold fibers. The fibrous texture of the paper has so much character that it is a shame to bury it under a thick polyurethane finish, as would usually be done for a bracelet. Instead, lightly coat the beads with a thin application of PVA glue, then string them on gold embroidery ribbon. The result is a colorful bracelet that is quite sophisticated and remarkably simple to make.

Materials

$\frac{3}{32}$" × 2" (2.5 mm × 5 cm) cotter pin

Scissors

Needle-nosed pliers

Ruler

Pencil

Embroidery needle

6 yards (5.5 meters) of $\frac{1}{8}$" (.3 cm) embroidery ribbon

Piece of gold threaded red paper, 10" × 7" (25 cm × 18 cm)

Spring ring clasp

Pair of 6 mm jump rings

Sewing needle

Cotton thread to match ribbon

$\frac{3}{4}$"
(2 cm)

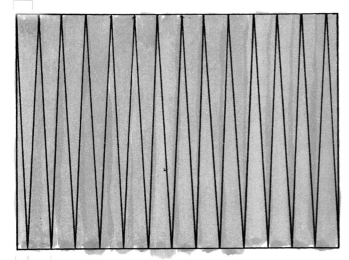

$\frac{3}{8}$" $\frac{3}{4}$" (2 cm)
(1 cm)

Getting Started

Turn the paper you have chosen to the "wrong" side (the side that will become the inside of the rolled-up bead) and make a pencil mark every $\frac{3}{4}$" (2 cm) down the 10" (25 cm) edge. On the opposite edge, make one mark $\frac{3}{8}$" (1 cm) from the edge of the paper, then make marks every $\frac{3}{4}$" (2 cm) for the length of the sheet. Use a ruler to connect the marked points in a zigzag fashion, then cut the paper into the resulting triangular strips. Discard the first and last pieces.

1 Wind twenty-four beads, following the instructions in How to Make Paper Beads on page 7. Use a drop of PVA glue to coat the beads and let them dry thoroughly.

2 Cut the embroidery ribbon into six, 1-yard (.9 meter) lengths and thread all six through the ring clasp, as shown. Center the clasp in the middle of the ribbon and knot the strands, pulling tight against the jump ring.

3 Separate the embroidery ribbon into three groups of four strands each. With an embroidery needle, thread a bead onto each set of ribbons and bring it all the way to the end of the strand.

4 Tie a knot after each bead by pulling the tail of the ribbon through the loop of the knot twice, as shown in the illustration. Push the knot firmly against the bead. Repeat steps 3 and 4 until you have strung and knotted eight beads onto each group of ribbons. Keep the ribbon tension taut, but not so tight that the beads buckle, and try to make knots that are the same size.

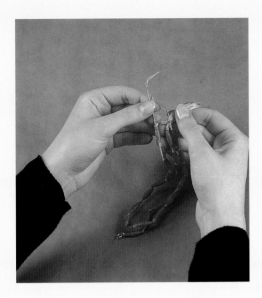

5 Thread all the ribbons through the middle of the jump ring. Then, working one bead strand at a time, use the embroidery needle to thread all four ribbons in each group back down through their corresponding knot and final bead. This secures the end of the ribbon.

6 With the sewing needle and thread, make two or three small stitches in the ribbon just below the final knot of each strand. This will further secure the back-tracking of the ribbons. Cut the remaining ribbon ends as close to the bead as you can.

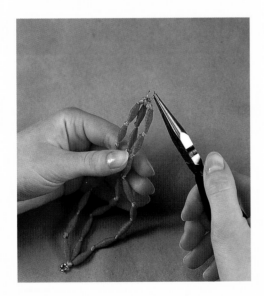

7 With the needle-nosed pliers, open the second jump ring slightly and link it with the first, using the pliers to close it again.

Variation
on a Theme

For this version of the project, $\frac{1}{2}$"(1 cm) beads were used in two colors and three different colored threads, instead of the three gold strands. The result is a beautiful collage of green and blue hues for a very attractive bracelet.

Flapper's Bead
Necklace

You will find this necklace effortless to assemble because embroidery floss is made of six individual threads that can be easily separated from one another. These threads are separated and then recombined in this piece to form the multiple strands. When you reach the point in the step-by-step instructions where the floss is threaded in three directions, you will separate the floss into three pairs of threads. When the instructions call for one strand again, you will thread all three pairs back through the needle.

Materials

2 pieces of Thai marbled paper, 6" × 24" (15 cm × 61 cm)

2 pieces of gold spotted maroon paper,
6" × 6 ¾" (15 cm × 17 cm) and
6" × 6" (15 cm × 15 cm)

³⁄₃₂" × 2" (2.5 mm × 5 cm) cotter pin

PVA glue

Water-based polyurethane

Small paintbrush

Gold barrel necklace clasp

2 pieces of 36" (91 cm) long black
embroidery floss

Ruler

Scissors

Embroidery needle

Pencil

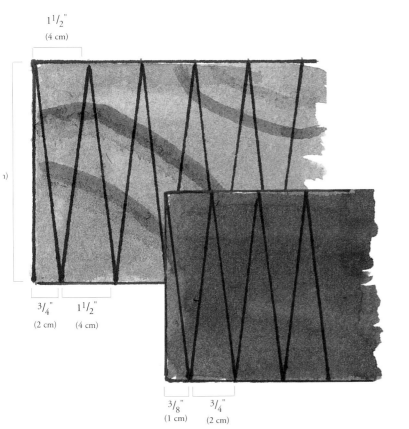

1½" (4 cm)

¾" (2 cm) 1½" (4 cm)

³⁄₈" (1 cm) ¾" (2 cm)

Getting Started

Review the section on How to Make Paper Beads on page 7. To make twenty-four *cylindrical* beads, start by cutting the 6" × 6 ¾" (15 cm × 17 cm) piece of maroon paper into twenty-four strips measuring ¼" × 6" (.5 cm × 15 cm). Follow the illustrations to make sixty-two Thai marbled paper *oval* beads and thirty-two maroon *oval* beads. Brush three coats of polyurethane over the beads, letting each coat dry before adding the next.

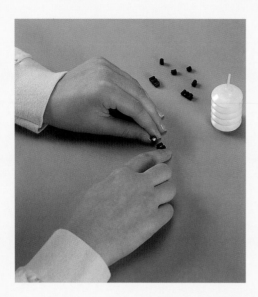

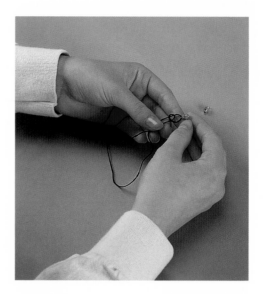

1 Line up three of the cylindrical beads side by side and use a dot of PVA glue between each bead to glue this grouping together. This will transform the three individual beads into a single bead with three thread holes. This triple bead will stabilize the multiple strands that make up this necklace.

2 To begin stringing the necklace, take one piece of the embroidery floss and tie the end to the ring on one side of the clasp, leaving a 3" (8 cm) tail. Thread the needle onto the floss. As you proceed to form the necklace, remember to keep the beads snug against each other, but not so tight that the necklace buckles.

3 Thread both the long section of floss and the tail through an oval maroon bead, a Thai bead, and another oval maroon bead. Continue stringing beads alternating oval maroon and Thai beads until a total of eight beads are on the strand, ending with a maroon bead. Separate the embroidery floss into three bundles of two threads each. Following the illustration, thread beads onto each of these bundles, then join all three threads back into a single bundle and thread back through an oval maroon bead, a Thai bead, and another maroon bead. Split the threads again into three bundles of two threads each, and continue the beading pattern as shown. At the end, remove the needle and set the piece aside.

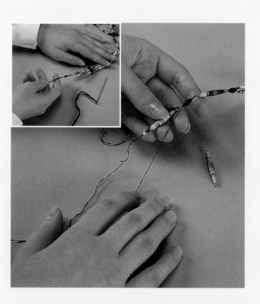

4 Repeat step 2 with the other piece of floss and the other side of the clasp and then follow step 3 to make the other side of the necklace.

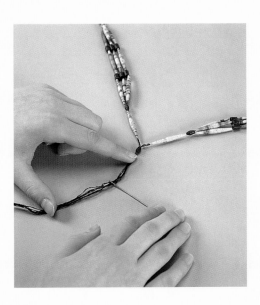

5 Thread the floss from both sides of the necklace through the needle and take this through one small maroon oval bead, joining the two sides together.

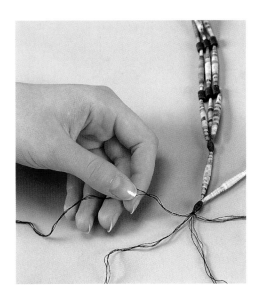

6 Remove the needle and separate the threads of the two pieces of floss into four groups of three threads each to prepare for the "tassel."

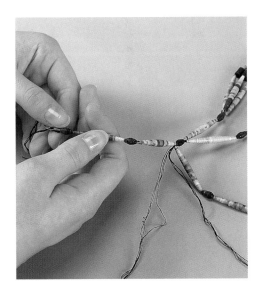

7 Take one of the groups back through the needle and string two marbled beads and two small maroon oval beads. Tie a knot or two in the end of the strand tight against the last bead. Thread the tail back through the last three beads and cut it off as close to the bead as possible. Repeat with the remaining three groups of thread.

Variation on a Theme

Make sure your necklace length is right for your proportions. This necklace is shorter than the one in the project but makes its statement with alternating bands of color. The beads are made by rolling a triangle of black paper laminated on top of a slightly larger silver foil triangle. Black embroidery floss and two strands of silver thread were knotted between beads.

17

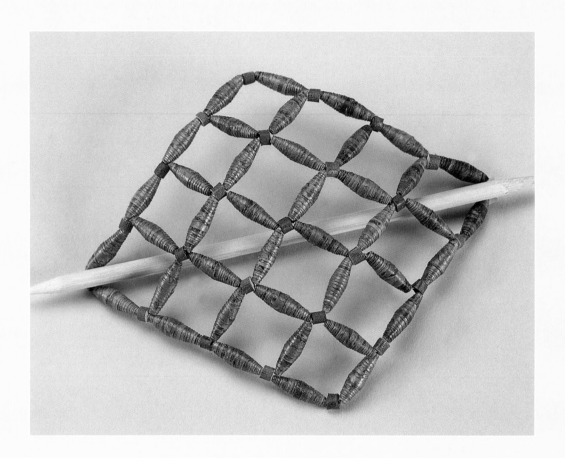

Paper Bead
Hair Slide

The deep colors of the beautiful gold floral wrapping paper used to make the beads for this project give it a medieval touch. This piece is an elegant way to put up your hair that is much less complicated to make than it looks. The key is to keep the beads snug up against each other as you work, following the simple instructions and illustrations. In just a matter of hours, you will be wearing a handmade masterpiece of timeless appeal.

Materials

Scissors

Ruler

Pencil

PVA glue

$^{3}/_{32}$" × 2" (2.5 mm × 5 cm) cotter pin

15 feet (460 cm) of 28-gauge brass wire

Piece of gold and floral wrapping paper,
   $6^{1}/_{2}$"× 16" (17 cm × 41 cm)

Piece of green paper, $1^{3}/_{4}$" × 2" (4.5 cm × 5 cm)

Piece of pink paper, $1^{3}/_{4}$" × 2" (4.5 cm × 5 cm)

$^{1}/_{4}$" (.5 cm) wooden dowel

Pencil sharpener

Small hand saw

Water-based polyurethane

Small paintbrush

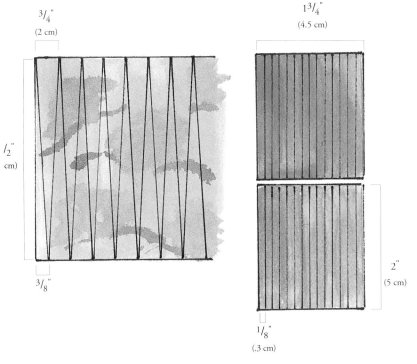

$3/_4$"
(2 cm)

$1^3/_4$"
(4.5 cm)

$/_2$"
cm)

$3/_8$"

2"
(5 cm)

$1/_8$"
(.3 cm)

Getting Started

Follow this illustration to cut out the paper strips.
Make forty oval gold beads by cutting the gold and
floral wrapping paper into long, triangular strips
measuring $6^{1}/_{2}$" × $^{3}/_{4}$" (17 cm × 2 cm). To make
the gold beads, as well as the thirteen, cylindrical $^{1}/_{8}$"
(.3 cm) green beads and the twelve, $^{1}/_{8}$" (.3 cm)
cylindrical pink beads, form the beads as directed in
How to Make Paper Beads on page 7. Add three
coats of polyurethane to each bead, allowing each
coat to dry before adding the next.

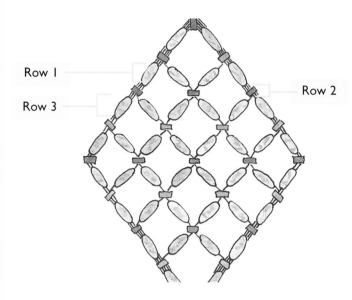

Row 1

Row 3

Row 2

1 Use the scissors to cut five, 3 foot (90 cm) pieces of wire, then thread all five pieces through one green bead. On both sides of the green bead, thread a gold and then a pink bead. Center this series of beads on the wires, then bend the wires in half at the green bead.

2 Beginning at row 1, follow the illustration to thread all the beads. It helps to hook your work over a nail to provide adequate tension. The first four wires of the left-hand packet are threaded through one gold bead, as is the remaining wire. From the right-hand packet of wires, one wire is threaded through one gold bead, and the next four wires are then threaded through a single gold bead.

3 Thread one set of five wires through one green bead. Thread the remaining five wires through the same green bead but in the opposite direction.

4 Pull all the wires around to the back side of the piece and twist them together once or twice. Work the first set of five wires back through one of the last gold beads. Repeat with the other five wires through the gold bead on the other side of the final green bead.

5 Use the scissors to trim the excess wire off as close as possible to the beads. You may find it helpful to bend the hair piece back so that you may cut the wires very close to the gold beads. Having done that, gently shape the piece into its proper diamond shape with a gentle convex curve.

6 Use the hand saw to cut a 6 ½" (17 cm) piece of the dowel, then sharpen each end of the dowel in the pencil sharpener until the point resembles the end of a chopstick.

Variation on a Theme

You can use the same basic techniques to make any number of shapes for other hair slides. In this hair piece, the beads are worked into a figure-eight pattern that requires only four wires instead of five. Wire is knotted between each bead just as the thread was in the Triple Strand Bracelet on page 10.

*I*t may be hard to believe, but the simple papier-mâché skills learned by children in grade school or at summer camp can be put to use creating elegant jewelry. Paper strips and wallpaper paste, both readily available and inexpensive materials, can be used to make a variety of professional-looking bracelets, necklaces, and pins.

The easiest papier-mâché method, strip papier-mâché, has only a few components when working on such small pieces as jewelry. Before beginning, make some sort of internal structure or skeleton for the project out of cardboard and/or wire; anything that creates the general outline of the finished product can be used. Once the skeleton is ready, layer it with strips of paper that have been dipped in thick liquid paste such as liquid starch or water-thinned white glue. The easiest glue to obtain and work with is wallpaper paste. It is sold in most hardware or paint and paper stores as a powder to which you add water to form the paste.

Papier-Mâché Jewelry

Just about any paper can be used to layer over your base shape.

Newspaper ripped into strips is the traditional choice, but any lightweight paper will work. Be careful of papers that are too thin—they will rip apart when soaked with the paste. On the other hand, very thick papers do not have the flexibility to wrap neatly around the skeleton of a piece. The choice depends on the finished look you are trying to achieve. The Celestial Bangle on page 34 uses the properties of lightweight tissue paper to create the texture on the surface of the pieces. A very large, flat, and chunky project, however, could benefit from robust, heavier papers.

The size of your project determines the size of the paper strips that you will need. Use short, narrow strips to cover the skeletons of jewelry shapes. Avoid having the paper fold over itself, adding unnecessary bulk to the piece. Choose the appropriate thickness of paper and tear it into the proper size strip to assure quick progress and a neat end result.

Another papier-mâché method, pulp papier-mâché, is quickly gaining in popularity, and many arts and crafts stores carry the mix. Paper is ground up and mixed with paste so that it has the consistency of clay. The pulp can be freely modeled into any shape or applied to a skeleton and dries very hard. Once dry, you can smooth the dappled surface by leveling it with spackle. Keep in mind that either form of papier-mâché can get messy, so protect your work surface by covering it with tin foil or wax paper, which won't stick to your project.

How to Make Strip Papier-Mâché

Materials

Wallpaper paste mixed as directed on
  its package

Paper torn into strips

Skeleton for your project

1 Dip a strip of paper into the paste and
then slide it through your fingers to
remove the excess.

2 Lay the strip over the skeleton,
neatly wrapping it around bends
and angles. Dip another strip and lay it
next to, but slightly overlapping, the
first. Continue laying down strips in
the same direction. Let each layer dry
thoroughly before adding the next.

3 Lay down the next layer of papier-
mâché with the strips perpendicular to
the first layer to strengthen the piece's
structure. For example, if the first layer
of papier-mâché traveled from left to right,
the next layer will travel from top to bottom.

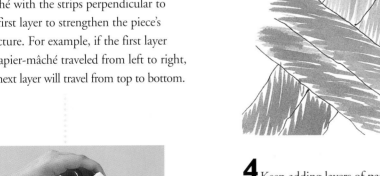

4 Keep adding layers of papier-mâché
until the paper skin is the appropriate
thickness. Remember to let each layer
dry thoroughly before adding the next,
alternating the direction of the strips
for each layer.

Recipe for Strip Papier-Mâché Paste

Ingredients

$1/3$ cup flour
2 cups cold water
Saucepan
Spoon

1 Mix the flour and the water together in
the pan and let it sit until there are no
lumps, about twenty minutes.

2 Place the pan over medium-high heat and
bring to a boil, stirring constantly.

3 Remove the pan from the heat and let the
paste cool before using.

Recipe for Pulp Papier-Mâché

Ingredients

Pulp papier-mâché mixed as
  directed on its package
Skeleton for the project
Spackle
Putty knife
Fine sandpaper

1 This one is easy! Working with small
amounts at a time, simply mold the pulp
around the skeleton, filling in the basic
shape. Cover the skeleton completely. For
small projects, an internal structure may not
be necessary; just model the pulp freely, like
clay, to form the general figure.

2 With more pulp, add the details (features,
curves) of the piece. Set it aside until completely dry. Drying time varies greatly
depending on the thickness of the piece.

3 For a very smooth finish, cover the surface
with a thin, no more than $1/8$" (.3 cm), layer
of spackle and drag the knife over it while it
is still wet, removing the excess. Don't leave
any ruts or ridges. The spackle that is left
behind fills in the low spots of the pulp surface. Once the spackle is dry (about an
hour), you can further smooth the surface
by lightly sanding it.

Like many people, I first encountered papier-mâché as a child. I remember being enthralled by the cool, thick paste I could squish between my fingers and the outlandish characters I could create so easily. My first project, a clown piñata for my seventh birthday party, was more funny looking than funny, but it introduced me to a technique that I used for other childhood projects, from an elephant head for Halloween to a volcano for science class.

Making the Jewelry

Once you have built the skeleton and skin of a project, use the last layer of strip papier-mâché or the wet papier-mâché pulp to achieve a vast number of looks and finishes. In strip papier-mâché, try using a different thickness of paper for the last layer. Fold or bunch the strips as you lay them down to add texture to the piece. Use colored paper for the final layer to eliminate the need to paint. For pulp papier-mâché, add dye to the pulp mixture. In addition, after modeling the pulp, try pressing flowers, buttons, or other found objects into the wet surface. The flower can either become part of the surface design or you can remove it to leave behind an impression of its petals and stamens.

Papier-Mâché Tips

Store unused *papier-mâché* in the refrigerator to extend its useful life.

Use *cookie cutters* as forms for pulp papier-mâché to make easy ornaments, charms, or pins.

Try using *materials* other than paper, such as fabrics or leaves, for the final layer of strip papier-mâché.

Cover your work *surface* with either tin foil or wax paper to keep your project from sticking to anything.

To make *unusual* and funky beads, form pulp papier-mâché into small shapes and push a needle through them while the pulp is still wet. Allow these to dry and then decorate as you desire with paints, glitter, or inks.

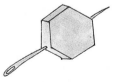

Before adding your *last layer* of papier-mâché, glue items such as spirals of string or cardboard cutouts to the surface to create texture and features in the finished surface.

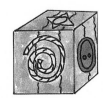

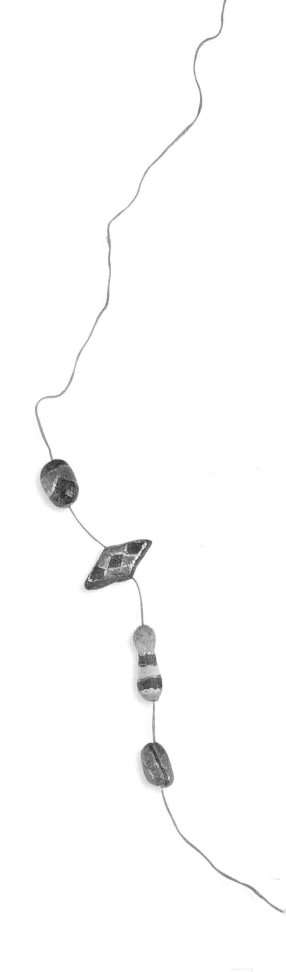

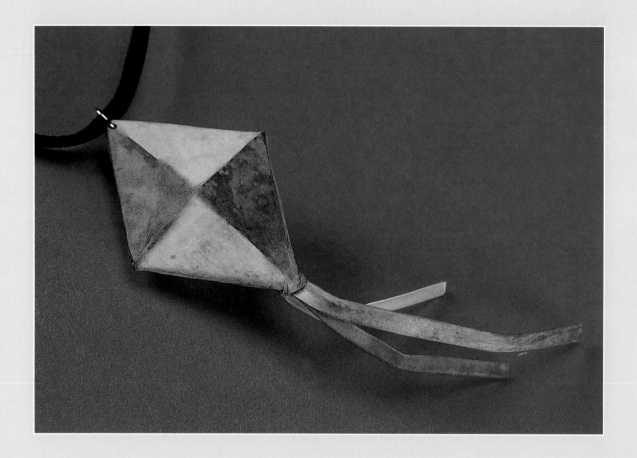

Kite
Pendant

The tails of this kite are wire, which can be bent to mimic wind blowing through them. The tissue papers are so thin that their colors become somewhat translucent when they are papiermâchéd in place, resulting in a beautiful blending of color in the finished piece.

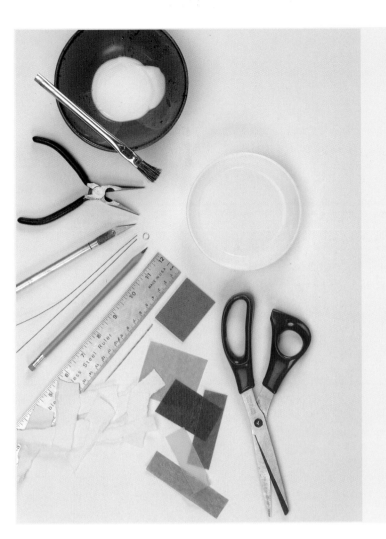

Materials

$\frac{1}{16}$" (1.5 mm) chipboard or cardboard
  measuring $1\frac{1}{2}$" × 2" (4 cm × 5 cm)

Sheet of white typing paper, cut into strips
  measuring $\frac{1}{2}$" × 7" (1 cm × 18 cm)

$7\frac{1}{2}$" (19 cm) of 26-gauge wire

Tissue paper: dark green, light green, pink,
  yellow, and blue

Wallpaper paste mixed as directed on its package

PVA glue

Glue brush

Embroidery needle

4 mm silver jump ring

Ruler

Pencil

Craft knife

Scissors

Needle-nosed pliers

Getting Started

With the ruler and the pencil, mark the midpoints of
each side of the rectangle of chipboard and draw lines
to connect them, forming a diamond. Use the craft
knife to cut out the diamond.

1 Line up the ruler to connect two opposite points of the diamond. Use the craft knife to score the front of the board, making sure to cut only halfway through its thickness. Repeat this between the other two points and bend the chipboard diamond back along both score lines so that a peak is formed in the middle of the diamond. This peaked side will be the front of the kite.

2 To make the tails of the kite, take a strip of white paper and spread a thin coat of glue over one side. Place the wire, lengthwise, in the center of the strip and fold the paper in half, enclosing the wire. This white paper will serve as a base for the very thin tissue paper.

3 Cut the paper-covered wire into three lengths: 3" (8 cm), 2½" (6 cm), and 2" (5 cm). Coat the 3" (8 cm) paper-covered wire with the wallpaper paste and cover it with the blue tissue paper. Do the same with the 2½" (6 cm) wire and the pink paper, and the 2" (5 cm) wire and the yellow paper. Set these aside to dry.

4 Use the scissors to trim the tails so that they are ⅛" (.3 cm) wide. Glue them to the back side of the bottom point of the kite. Be sure that you are using the pieces with the wire inside them.

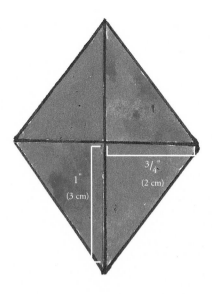

5 With the remaining white paper strips, cover the chipboard with two layers of papier-mâché. Remember to let the first layer of papier-mâché dry before adding the second and that the second layer should be laid down perpendicular to the first. Use the light green tissue paper as a final third layer of papier-mâché.

6 Cut out two triangles of dark green tissue paper according to the dimensions in the illustration and papier-mâché them in place as shown.

7 With the needle, punch a hole in the top point of the kite. Use the needle-nosed pliers to thread the jump ring through the hole. Bend the tails into shape so that they look as though the wind is blowing through them.

Variation on a Theme

This leaf pendant uses a wire armature like the kite tails to give it its shape. To form the features of the leaf, use the pulp papier-mâché instead of the strip papier-mâché method.

Fishy *Pulp Pins*

These charming pins could not be any easier to make! Pulp papier-mâché allows this project
to progress quickly and provides you with an end result that will endure time, wear, and the
elements (even water). You can use bright colors to decorate the fish for your lapel or bag, or, if
you prefer a more subdued finish, try painting in tones of blue and green. Either way, these
aquatic creatures are simple projects that can be used as beautiful jewelry.

Materials

PVA glue

Spackle

Putty knife

Black, white, red, yellow, and green latex paint

Paintbrush

Wax paper

Pulp papier-mâché

Sandpaper

Two 1" (3 cm) pin backs

Water-based polyurethane

Indelible black marker

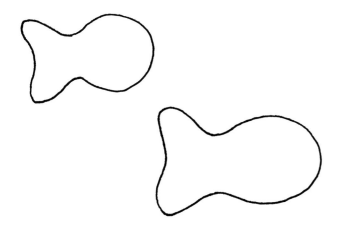

Getting Started

Transfer the fish patterns to the wax paper using the carbon paper method described in How to Transfer Images and Patterns, page 40.

1 Place a small amount of pulp into the outline of one fish and flatten it until it is about ¼" (.5 cm) thick, keeping the pulp within the lines. Continue adding pulp until the entire silhouette is filled in. Repeat with the other fish.

2 Add a little more pulp to the head and tail of one fish so that it is slightly mounded. Gently mold the pulp to define the shape of the fish, smoothing out any rough spots in the surface of the pulp. Repeat with the other fish and set the two aside overnight or until they are thoroughly dry.

3 To create a very smooth finish, spackle and sand the fish using the technique described in step 3 of the Recipe for Pulp Papier-Mâché on page 23.

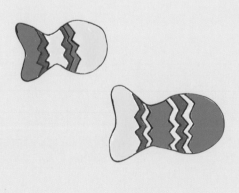

4 Following the pattern, paint the background colors of each fish and set them aside to dry for about an hour.

5 Using the red, black, and white paint, add the mouth and eyes. When the paint is dry (approximately one hour), use the indelible marker to add the outlines. Apply three coats of polyurethane to the front and back of each fish, letting each coat dry before adding the next.

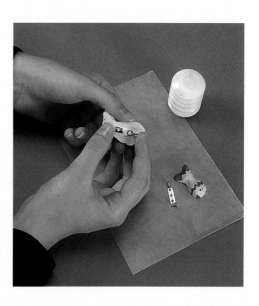

6 Once the polyurethane is dry, run a bead of glue onto one 1" (3 cm) pin back and press it firmly onto the back of one fish. Repeat with the other.

Variation
on a Theme

Molding pulp papier-mâché is so easy that any number of characters can quickly and easily come to life. This emerald toad is fashioned just like the fish.

Celestial Bangle *Bracelet*

The magical realm of the night sky is captured in this lighthearted bangle bracelet. The real wonder, though, is how easy it is to use papier-mâché to create it. The skeleton is made of chipboard squares, covered by strip papier-mâché. Tissue paper, wrinkled to add texture and character to the finished piece, is used as the last papier-mâché layer. When the gold ink is added, you will find that the wrinkles on the tissue paper will add to the weathered look of the final bracelet.

Materials

Pencil

Needle-nosed pliers

Piece of $\frac{1}{16}$" (1.5 mm) chipboard or
    cardboard, 4" × 4" (10 cm × 10 cm)

Ruler

Craft knife

Wallpaper paste mixed as directed on its package

White paper strips, $\frac{1}{2}$" × 2" (1 cm × 5 cm)

Sturdy scissors

PVA glue

Glue brush

Tissue paper strips, 1" × $1\frac{1}{2}$" (3 cm × 4 cm)

Small paintbrush

Purple latex paint

Gold pen

Embroidery needle

Water-based polyurethane

18 gold 7 mm jump rings

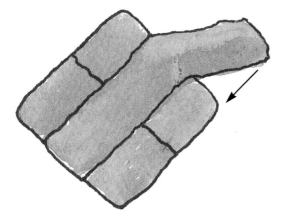

Lay down the second layer perpendicular to the first.

Getting Started

With the ruler and craft knife, cut eight 1"
(3 cm) squares from the chipboard. Cover the
squares with two layers of papier-mâché each
made from the white paper, following the basic
directions given in How to Make Strip Papier-
Mâché on page 23. Remember to lay down the
second layer of papier-mâché perpendicular to
the first.

1 On the remaining piece of chipboard, draw an assortment of four stars and four moons, making sure that their dimensions do not exceed $3/4$" (2 cm) in any direction. You may find it useful to draw a grid on the board first so that you can draw the stars and moon within them. Use the scissors to cut them out, then glue one to the center of each square made in Getting Started.

2 Dip a strip of tissue paper into the papier-mâché paste and wrap it around a square. Allow it to wrinkle and fold over itself to give the piece some texture. Make sure, though, that the shape (star or moon) is still well defined. Continue adding tissue paper strips in a single layer until the entire square is covered. Repeat this process with the remaining seven squares.

3 After a few hours, when the papier-mâché is thoroughly dry, apply a thin coat of purple paint to one side of each of the squares. When this is dry, in about thirty minutes, paint the other side of the squares with the same color.

4 When the paint is dry, use the gold pen to outline the squares and to color in the shapes themselves. For a weathered look, partially color in the shapes and use your finger to spread the wet ink. To finish the square, apply two coats of polyurethane with a small brush, allowing the first to dry at least an hour before adding the second.

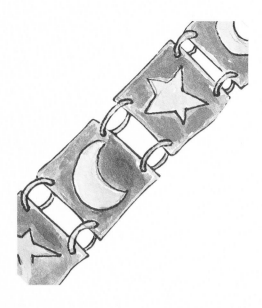

5 Use the needle to punch holes in all the squares as shown. When all eight pieces have been punched, you are ready to form the bracelet.

6 Line up the squares in front of you, alternating moons and stars. Use the needle-nosed pliers to open the jump rings to connect each square to the next as shown.

7 When all the pieces have been attached to each other, gently curve the bracelet into a circle and use the last two jump rings to secure the first square to the last.

Variation on a Theme

Bangles look great no matter what shape their pieces are, but simply changing the location of where the pieces join can dramatically alter the look of the piece. For this red version of the bracelet, squares are joined at their corner points instead of along their edges.

$\mathcal{D}$ecoupage, the use of paper cutouts to cover a surface, began in eighteenth-century France, when court ladies tried to mimic popular Japanese and Chinese lacquered furniture of the era. The technique is still popular today because it is easy, and the results can be elegant. Decoupage jewelry is a beautiful way to display tiny pictures that would otherwise be too small to appreciate. A single cut image, such as a rose or a bird, can become an eye-catching pin or barrette. More intricate collages make both meaningful and beautiful pins or lockets.

There are only a few basics needed for a decoupage project. Choose a surface to decorate, then decide which images to cover it. Magazines, newspapers, and catalogs are good sources; even old books and photographs can be used. If cutting up treasured photos is unthinkable, modern photocopying techniques can give you a quality reproduction.

Decoupage Jewelry

Collecting and cutting out the pictures you want to use for jewelry is the most time-consuming aspect of the decoupage process, but the selection and arrangement of these cutouts will determine the success of the project. When you are choosing images, make sure their size is appropriate to the decorating surface. Large cutouts will feel heavy and may even seem to disappear as they wrap around the edges of a small piece. Small cutouts may be hard to appreciate, especially on large pieces. Play with the images to see how they best fit together. Once you have found an arrangement that suits your project, use a pencil to lightly outline where each piece goes on the background. This will make it easier to position the piece after you have brushed the glue on the back of it. When all the elements have been affixed to the background, several coats of lacquer are applied to create a polished, smooth surface.

How to Decoupage

Decoupage is fun and easy and can be tailored to suit anyone's interests, so choose a theme that appeals to you or the recipient of the piece you are making.

Materials

Assorted images

Scissors or craft knife

PVA glue

Tweezers

Glue brush

Water-based polyurethane or acrylic medium

Paintbrush

1 Begin by gathering an assortment of images that go well together. Once you have selected the pictures, carefully cut them out with either the scissors or the craft knife, following the outlines of the pictures exactly. Try to angle your cuts away from the image so that the top surface of the picture does not show the cut edge.

2 Lay out the pieces on the decorating surface and move them around, until you find an arrangement that appeals to you. Glue the background pictures first. Brush a thin coat of glue on the back of each and use the tweezers to lay them in place. Repeat this with each picture, beginning with background images and working toward those in the foreground. Set the entire piece aside to dry.

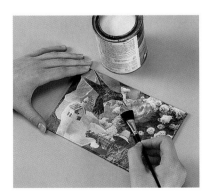

3 Brush multiple coats of polyurethane or acrylic medium over the decoupage, allowing each layer to dry for about an hour and a half before adding the next. Your goal is a smooth surface. Acrylic medium requires fewer coats than polyurethane, but both add a perfect finish. The number of coats required depends on the thickness of the cutout paper and the number of overlapping images involved. You may need five to twenty coats of finish.

How to Make Acrylic Transfers

Materials

Acrylic medium

Brush

Picture to be transferred

Flat, shallow pan of water

Wax paper

1 Place the picture on the wax paper, face up, and brush a coat of acrylic medium over it. Make sure that the medium extends all the way to the edges and that your brush strokes are all in the same direction. Set this aside to dry for one hour.

2 Brush a second coat of acrylic medium over the picture with the strokes moving perpendicular to those of the first coat. Set this aside to dry.

3 Repeat steps 1 and 2 until you have at least ten coats of acrylic medium over the picture.

4 Once the last coat of acrylic medium is dry (about one hour), place the whole piece in a pan of water and let it soak long enough that the paper absorbs some water and starts to soften. Depending on the paper, you may need to let it sit between fifteen and forty-five minutes.

5 With the piece face down in the water, start rubbing away the paper from the back with your fingers. Keep on rubbing, gently so as not to tear the film, until all the paper has been removed. Take the acrylic film out of the water, set aside to dry for a half an hour, and then use as desired for your project.

$\mathcal{D}$ecoupage is a simple technique, but it can be used to make ingenious necklaces, bracelets, earrings, and pins. Instead of using pictures that are picked out from a magazine, try cutting various colored papers into an assortment of shapes to assemble into a new, original image of your own. The Lady Pin is an example of how ordinary scraps of paper can be cut and formed into a beautiful piece. The cuff bracelet in this chapter uses a process of transferring images on paper to acrylic film, which is then cut to fit the decoupage. This film is created by brushing multiple layers of acrylic medium over the picture and soaking the piece in water so that the paper can be rubbed off. What remains is a film that holds only the colors of the original. The film can be stretched or otherwise manipulated and is so thin that its edges are difficult to detect beneath the finish coats of the project. Thanks to modern technology, treasured photo- graphs can be used in decoupage jewelry without damaging the original photo by making high-quality photocopies. The Floral Decoupage Locket uses a quick and easy transfer technique to create a silhouette from a photo. Once images are reproduced on white paper, they can be manipulated much more easily.

Making the Jewelry

Decoupage Tips

Photocopy your *favorite* photos to cut out images for decoupage.

To create a *crackle glaze* finish on your decoupage, brush thick layers of finish over the piece and apply the next before the previous has dried completely.

Add years to *the look* of your jewelry by using an oil-based polyurethane instead of a water-based one. The oil will add a yellowed tinge to the colors.

Lightly *sand* down the back of images on very thick paper. This will make them easier to work with in the decoupage.

Use *tweezers* to hold and place small pieces more easily.

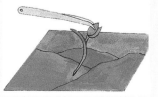

Carbon *paper* can be easily found in department stores and office supply stores.

How to Transfer Images and Patterns

Materials

Pattern

Fine point black indelible marker

Tracing paper

Carbon paper

Paper that the image is being transferred to

1 Choose an image or a pattern with clear, discernible edges, such as people, florals, animals, or furniture.

2 Place the tracing paper over the image and, with the marker, trace the pattern.

3 Lay the paper that the image is being transferred to face down in front of you. Place the carbon paper, ink side down, on top of that, and then the tracing, face down, on top of that.

4 Use the marker to retrace the pattern on the back side of the tracing paper, pushing down firmly so that the carbon paper is sure to leave its mark.

5 When you remove the tracing and carbon papers, you will see that the reverse of the original pattern is on the back side of your final paper. Once this is cut out, when you view the piece from the front side, you will have an exact replica of the pattern without any tracing lines showing.

Golden Ivy *Earrings*

These golden botanicals put a twist on the traditional decoupage technique; the paper cutouts of ivy leaves are mounted on wire so that they decorate space instead of a surface. The wire allows the leaves to be individually placed in their setting, and the gold gilt adds a touch of elegance to an earthy subject. This project can inspire a multitude of variations; you need look only as far as the garden to see what other climbing or draping plants would easily lend their likeness to this form.

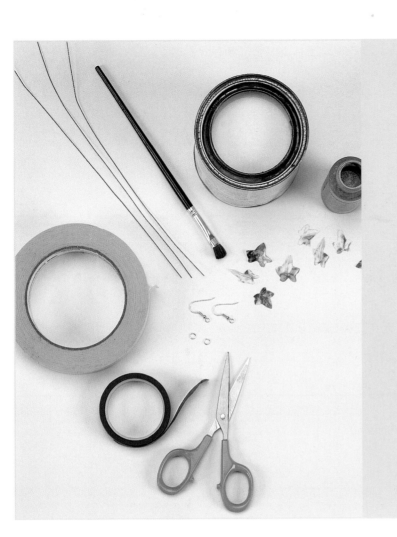

Materials

Cutouts of 8 gold ivy leaves

26" (66 cm) of 26-gauge wire

Floral tape

Scissors

Gold paint

Paintbrush

Earring hooks

1" (3 cm) wide masking tape

2 gold 4 mm jump rings

Water-based polyurethane

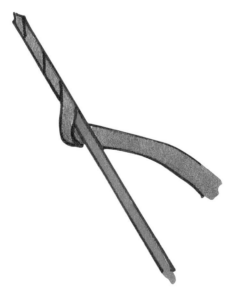

Getting Started

To create the stems, cut the wire into eight 3" (8 cm) lengths and wrap each piece with the floral tape, a stretchy green tape used by florists for wrapping wired stems and readily available at craft supply stores.

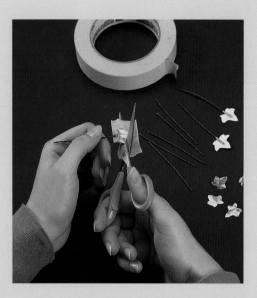

1 Use the masking tape to secure a piece of covered wire to the back of a leaf, making sure that the tape completely covers the back of the leaf. Turn the piece to the front side and use the scissors to trim off the over-hanging tape. Repeat with the other seven leaves.

2 Paint the back side of each leaf and its stem with the gold paint. When the paint is dry, brush a coat of polyurethane over the front, back, and stem of each piece. Set these aside to dry.

3 For one earring, cut the stems of four leaves down to 1 1/4" (4 cm), 1" (3 cm), 3/4" (2 cm), and 1/4" (1 cm). Set aside the leaf with the shortest stem and stack the other three on top of each other, lining up the stem ends. Each leaf should be staggered. Twist the ends of the stems together to secure. Repeat this step for the other earring.

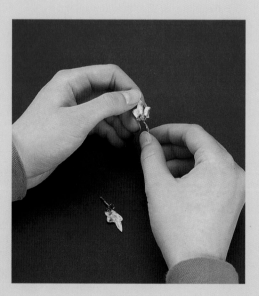

4 From the remaining unwrapped wire, cut a piece 1" (3 cm) long and insert it through one jump ring. Bend the wire in half, enclosing the jump ring. Place this piece on top of one remaining short-stemmed leaf, lining up the base of the leaf with the base of the jump ring. Twist the wires and the stem together. Repeat this process with the other jump ring and short-stemmed leaf.

5 As shown in the photo, place the jump ring and short-stemmed leaf on top of a stack of three leaves, with the short-stemmed leaf face down and the wires pointing downward, toward the leaves of the larger stack. Secure these pieces in place by wrapping the stack with a band of the floral tape. Repeat with the other set of leaves and wired jump ring for the other earring.

6 Use the paint to turn the green bands of floral tape holding together all the leaves into gold. When the paint is dry (about one hour), bend the top leaf of each earring forward to reveal its front side and hide the point where all the stems are held together. Gently bend the stems of each leaf forward and to one side or the other to make a natural looking ivy formation. Repeat with the other earring.

7 With the needle-nosed pliers, open the jump ring of one earring and slip it through one ear hook before closing the ring again. Repeat with the other earring.

Variation on a Theme

This delicate cluster of garlic flowers uses the same decoupage technique as the Golden Ivy Earrings on page 42. The flexible wire stems can be molded into a variety of shapes.

Lady *Pin*

It can be difficult to throw away those special scraps left over from other projects. Out of desperation to find use for these valued small pieces, I designed a whole line of whimsical pins including everything from flying pigs to French clowns. The young woman featured in this project turned out to be one of the most popular characters and is both easy and fun to make. The only difference between this and traditional decoupage is that you will be cutting out a pattern as opposed to a preexisting image. The application techniques involved are the same.

Materials

Piece of $\frac{1}{32}$" (.75 mm) chipboard or cardboard, 2" × 3" (5 cm × 8 cm)

Blue marbled paper for the suit

Brown marbled paper for the face and hands

Navy marbled paper for the shoes

Purple marbled paper for the belt

Black paper for the back of the pin

Craft knife

PVA glue

Glue brush

Water-based polyurethane

Black fine point indelible marker

Metallic gold marker

Small brush for polyurethane

Tweezers (optional)

1" (3 cm) pin back

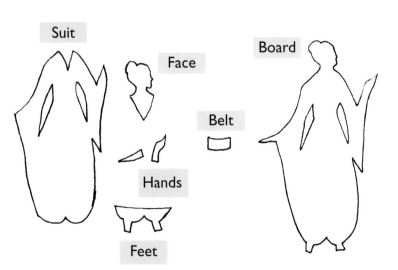

Getting Started

Use a photocopier to enlarge this pattern to fit on your piece of cardboard. Transfer the patterns to the papers as listed in Materials, and to the board, using the method described in How to Transfer Images and Patterns on page 40. Cut out all the pieces with the craft knife.

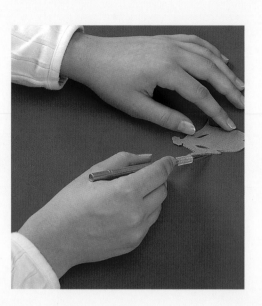

1 Attach the paper pieces of the lady's face to the cardboard backing by brushing a thin coat of glue on the back of the paper piece and press it into place on the front side of the cardboard. Glue each of the pattern pieces continuing in the following order: hands, feet, suit, and belt. Use the tweezers to hold onto and place small pieces.

2 Once all the pieces are glued in place, trim away any paper that overhangs the backing by flipping over the figure and running the knife blade along the edge of the cardboard.

3 Brush a thin coat of glue on the back of the figure and press it down firmly onto the back of the black paper. Trace around the edges of the woman with the knife to trim off any excess paper.

4 Use the marker to outline all the pieces that make up the figure, adding such detail as the facial features and clothing definition. The pattern shows the basics, but feel free to further embellish your pin as your creativity dictates. With the marker, blacken the edge all the way around the pin.

5 Apply three coats of polyurethane to the pin, making sure that the edges and back are coated as well. As always, make sure each coat has thoroughly dried (about an hour) before adding the next.

6 For the final step, spread a bit of glue on the top side of the 1" (3 cm) metal pin back and press it firmly onto the back side of the lady. Set this aside until it is thoroughly dry.

Variation
on a Theme

Any figure or shape can be made into a beautiful and colorful pin. Use the same cut paper process to make this angel pin or any other shape. Marbled papers are perfect for an angel pin, given their ethereal swirls.

Bronze and Lace
Cuff Bracelet

The secret to this unusual bracelet is an acrylic transfer of the lace image, backed with silver foil to make it sparkle. To learn how to transfer the lace image, see How to Make Acrylic Transfers on page 39. Real lace under the tissue paper covering the bracelet gives texture to the surface of the piece and highlights the lace pattern. Brush a coat of glue over the brown tissue paper covering the cuff bracelet to give it a metallic sheen. To assure that the bracelet keeps its shape, the chipboard is backed with several pieces of wire.

Materials

Piece of ¹⁄₃₂" (.75 mm) chipboard or cardboard, 2" × 7" (5 cm × 18 cm)

31" (79 cm) of 22-gauge wire

Masking tape

Sheet of brown tissue paper

Small square of silver foil paper

Scissors

Pencil

Metallic gold marker

Ruler

PVA glue

Glue brush

Small dish of water

Acrylic transfer of a lace image

Piece of lace, 1" × 5" (3 cm x 13 cm)

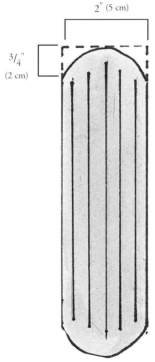

2" (5 cm)

3/4" (2 cm)

Getting Started

Trim the corners of the chipboard to create an elongated oval shape as shown. Cut the wire into two lengths of 6 ¼" (16 cm), two lengths of 6" (15 cm), and one length of 6 ½" (17 cm). Use masking tape to secure the entire length of each piece of wire to the chipboard in the following order: 6" (15 cm), 6 ¼" (16 cm), 6 ½" (17 cm), 6 ¼" (16 cm), and 6" (15 cm). The side with these wires will be the inside of the bracelet.

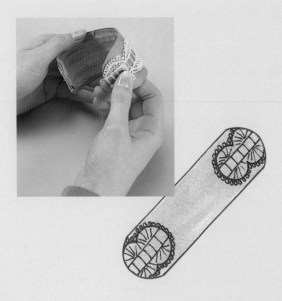

1 Cut two pieces of lace measuring 2 ¼" (6 cm) each and glue one down at each end of the oval chipboard, on the side without the wire, centering it between the long sides as shown in the illustration. Repeat with the other piece of lace on the other end. Gently bend the chipboard, wire side in, into a circular shape, being sure to leave at least a ¾" (2 cm) gap between the ends.

2 It is easier to work with the tissue if you thin the glue by dipping the glue brush in water before dipping it in the glue. Brush a thin coat of the glue and water mixture onto the surface of the bracelet. Lay down an 8" × 3" (20 cm × 8 cm) piece of tissue paper over the cuff, allowing it to slightly wrinkle and fold. Work it into the lace so that the pattern is clearly visible.

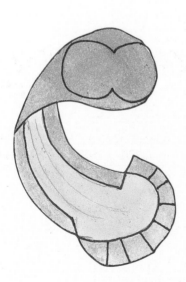

3 Clip the curves of the tissue paper extending beyond the edges of the chipboard as shown in the illustration. Brush a thin coat of glue around the inside edge of the bracelet and fold the tissue paper over to the inside. Make sure the tabs are pulled in firmly against the cardboard. Also be sure to fold in the long straight tabs on either side of the bracelet.

4 Cut a piece of tissue paper measuring 6 ½" × 1 ½" (17 cm × 4 cm) and round off the corners as you did the chipboard in step 1. Brush a thin coat of glue and water over the inside of the cuff and carefully lay the tissue paper into place. Brush a bit more glue and water over the entire surface of the cuff. This will give the cuff bracelet its metallic sheen.

5 Use the glue to secure the acrylic transfer to the silver foil and then carefully cut around the image of the lace. Glue this piece to the front of the cuff in the exact center.

6 From the edge of the tissue paper, cut two strips measuring ½" (1 cm) wide. Twist them together into a string as shown in the Origami Fold Bracelet step-by-step on page 68, and then glue the string around the edge of the lace acrylic transfer, framing the image. Trim off any excess string.

7 With the gold marker, draw a border all the way around the outside edge of the cuff. Draw over the outline of one piece of lace and, while the ink is still wet, smear it with your finger to give the cuff a weathered look. Repeat with the other piece of lace and the string frame around the transfer as well.

Variation
on a Theme

Cuff bracelets can take any shape or form; the basic construction remains the same. This puzzler takes its clues from the daily crosswords.

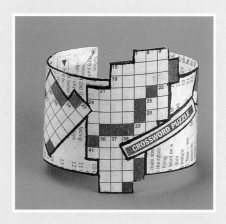

Floral Decoupage
Locket

My love for flowers became the subject of this elegant locket, but it is within the floral walls that the true value of this piece lies hidden: open the locket to reveal the silhouette of a very special person. To make the silhouette, a photograph of your subject becomes the pattern that you transfer using the carbon paper technique described in How to Transfer Images and Patterns on page 40. The solid color silhouette is reminiscent of an antique cameo and lends an heirloom air to the piece. For a more realistic approach, photocopy the photograph and cut out the image of your locket's featured character.

Materials

Needle-nosed pliers

Tweezers

Scissors

Small piece of $\frac{1}{16}$" (1.5 mm) chipboard or cardboard

PVA glue

Glue brush

Water-based polyurethane or acrylic medium

Masking tape

White paper for papier-mâché torn into strips

Papier-mâché paste mixed as directed on its package

Craft knife

Ruler

Pencil

Gold marker

2 gold 7 mm jump rings

Red tassel

Floral cutouts of images to decorate the locket

Yellow latex paint

Small paintbrush

Silhouette of a special friend cut out from heavy
    white paper

Embroidery needle

Getting Started

Out of the chipboard, cut two $1\frac{1}{2}$" (4 cm) squares and four triangular pieces, each $1\frac{1}{2}$" (4 cm) long and $\frac{3}{8}$" (1 cm) wide at the base. Cut out the pieces with the craft knife, using the ruler as a straight edge. Line up the ruler on the diagonal of each square, and use the knife to cut halfway through the thickness of the board from corner to corner. Cut only one diagonal on each square.

Score line

Front and Back
Cut 2

Sides
Cut 4

$1\frac{1}{2}$"
(4 cm)

$1\frac{1}{2}$"
(4 cm)

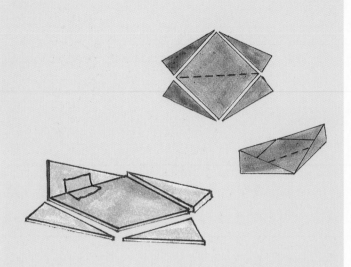

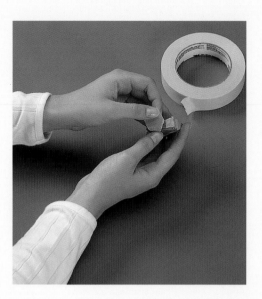

1 Lay the pieces out according to the illustration. One square piece should be placed scored side down, with the score traveling from left to right. Stand a triangle on its side edge, perpendicular to the adjoining edge of the square. Use the masking tape to secure it in place, taping it on both the inside and outside. Repeat with the three remaining triangles.

2 Gently fold the square along the score until the short edges of the adjacent triangles meet. Secure them in place with the masking tape. To complete the box, fold the second square over the top of the piece you just made, being sure that the score marks are pointed in the same direction for both squares. Fix the second square in place with tape.

3 Now that the skeleton of your locket is made, the "skin" must be created. With the white paper, apply three layers of papier-mâché over the box of the locket following the instructions given in How to Make Strip Papier-Mâché on page 23. Remember to allow each layer to dry a few hours before adding the next.

4 When the papier-mâché is thoroughly dry, orient the locket so that a corner of the square where two triangle points meet is situated at the top. Add the decoupage using the method described in How to Decoupage on page 39. When the glue is dry, apply five coats of either polyurethane or acrylic medium. As always, wait for each coat to dry before applying the next.

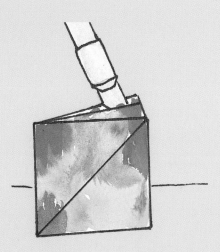

5 Use the knife to cut the locket in half all the way around the middle of the triangular sides. It may be helpful to first mark your cutting line lightly with pencil, and then place the locket on the edge on your work surface and cut it as you would a bagel.

6 Add a very neat layer of papier-mâché to the inside of the locket. When it is dry, brush on a coat of the yellow paint and then, when dry, a coat of polyurethane or acrylic medium.

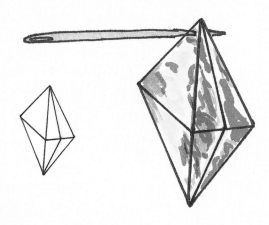

7 Hold the front and back of the locket in the "closed" position, and with the gold marker, draw a line on either side of the cut made earlier. Use the embroidery needle to punch a hole through the top point of the locket ⅛" (.3 cm) from the sides. Thread a jump ring through both the sides with the needle-nosed pliers. This ring will serve as the hinge for the locket.

8 In the bottom point of the front side only, punch another hole. Thread a jump ring through the hole and tie the tassel to the ring. Glue your silhouette inside the center back of the locket. String some silk cording or a favorite necklace through the hinge of the locket and try it on.

*T*he playful creatures and fanciful designs created by paper folding and weaving have entertained generations. These two techniques can also make very modern objects of beauty and function, such as jewelry, that are surprisingly easy to make and durable.

Folding paper is not a complicated skill. However, to assure very neat and professional-looking results, use a ruler to take careful measurements. It also helps to pre-bend the fibers of the paper along the fold line, so that the fold will be placed accurately without any wrinkling or bunching. This is done by lining up the ruler between the two end points of the fold and running the blade of a butter knife between these points. The number of layers in the final piece is naturally increased as the paper is folded back on itself to create the desired pattern; this is what will give the jewelry its strength. The more layers of paper, the stronger the piece will be. For this reason, be careful when choosing the papers for your projects. A thick paper will not accept multiple folds and still give clean, neat, or accurate results.

Woven and Folded Paper Jewelry

Paper weaving is a wonderfully simple way to achieve a multi-colored and textural piece of art. The basic materials involve only some strips of paper to weave together. A portion of these strips is lined up side by side to create the warp of your weaving, traveling from top to bottom. The remaining strips of paper are the weft of the weaving and will travel horizontally over the first warp strip and under the next, continuing across the width of the piece in this pattern. The next weft (horizontal) strip does the opposite of the first, going under the first warp strip and over the next. The weaving gets its strength from the intersection of the warp and weft strips that gives a double layer of paper twice as strong as the original single thickness of paper.

Weaving and folding are both such simple techniques that you will quickly master them. What is so surprising is that such basic skills can produce a multitude of variations in pattern. With a little experimentation, you are sure to discover a wide variety of options to add to your design palette.

How to Basket Weave

The basket weave is the most basic of weaving styles. Not only quick and easy, it is a beautiful design that has a multitude of variations.

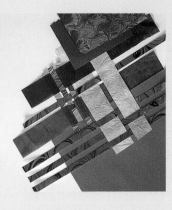

Materials

7 strips of pink paper

7 strips of yellow paper

Clipboard

1 Line up the pink strips of paper, side by side, and slip their tops under the clip of the clipboard. These strips will make up the warp of your weaving.

2 The yellow strips are the weft of your piece and will travel from right to left (or left to right). Starting with one, thread it under the first pink strip and over the next. Continue in this under/over pattern across the piece. Push the strip up against the clip of the board.

3 With another yellow strip, weave across the pink strips in the same under/over pattern, but this time start by going over the first pink strip. Push this piece firmly against the first strip you wove.

4 Repeat steps 2 and 3 for the length of the weaving.

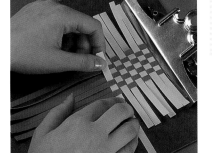

For neat, clean folds, it is important to pre-bend the fibers of the paper along the fold line. Follow these three easy steps, and you are sure to be pleased with the results of your paper folding project.

Materials

Ruler

Pencil

Butter knife

Folding paper project

1 Carefully measure and mark off the endpoints of the fold on the side of the paper that will be hidden inside the final fold.

2 Line up the ruler between the two endpoints, and run the blade of the butter knife along its edge, creating an impression of a line.

3 Fold the paper over and crease it along the fold line you just made. Remember the fold line marked on the paper is always on the inside of the fold. For your work to progress efficiently, pre-bend the fibers along all the fold lines in the project before going back to fold them all.

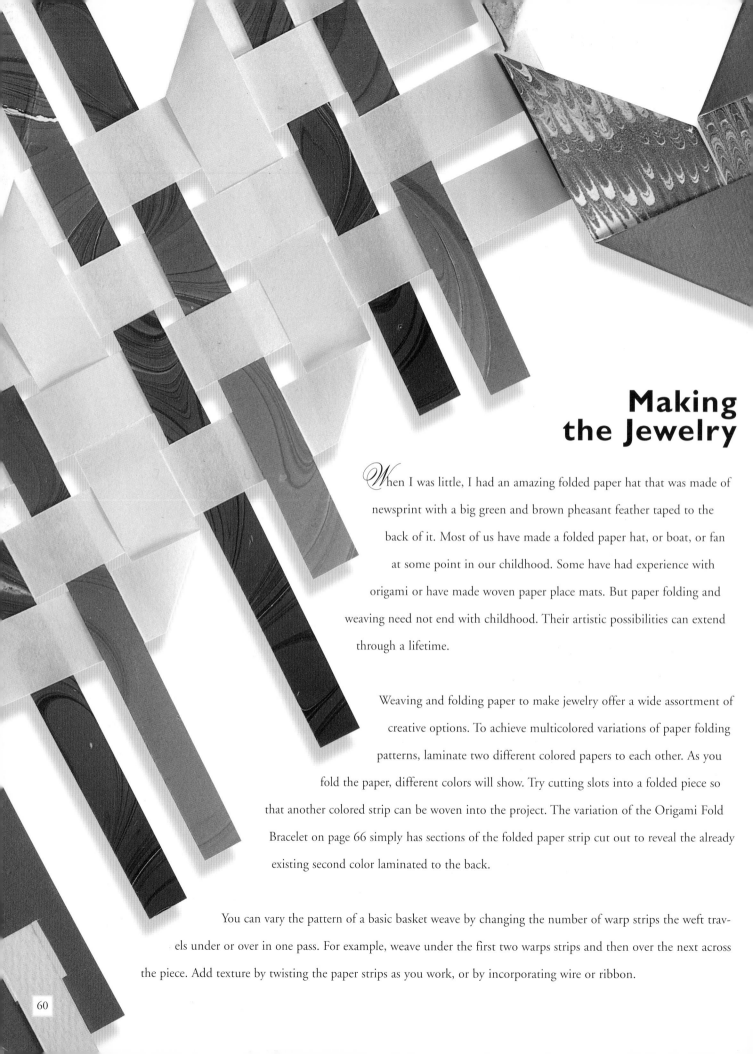

Making the Jewelry

When I was little, I had an amazing folded paper hat that was made of newsprint with a big green and brown pheasant feather taped to the back of it. Most of us have made a folded paper hat, or boat, or fan at some point in our childhood. Some have had experience with origami or have made woven paper place mats. But paper folding and weaving need not end with childhood. Their artistic possibilities can extend through a lifetime.

Weaving and folding paper to make jewelry offer a wide assortment of creative options. To achieve multicolored variations of paper folding patterns, laminate two different colored papers to each other. As you fold the paper, different colors will show. Try cutting slots into a folded piece so that another colored strip can be woven into the project. The variation of the Origami Fold Bracelet on page 66 simply has sections of the folded paper strip cut out to reveal the already existing second color laminated to the back.

You can vary the pattern of a basic basket weave by changing the number of warp strips the weft travels under or over in one pass. For example, weave under the first two warps strips and then over the next across the piece. Add texture by twisting the paper strips as you work, or by incorporating wire or ribbon.

Folding Tips

Folding, *combined* with a little bit of cutting, can create some playful pop-ups for lockets.

Cut out *portions* of a woven or folded piece to reveal other colors or images you affix to their backs.

Make small *origami* creatures to use for earrings, pendants, or charms.

After *folding* a number of paper strips into a patterned strap, weave these pieces together to create a colorful and/or textural visual.

Leave some *space* between each of the warp strips and each of the weft strips. These openings in the weaving will give the piece a lacy look.

For *weavings* with a more earthy look, tear your strips instead of giving them a neatly cut edge.

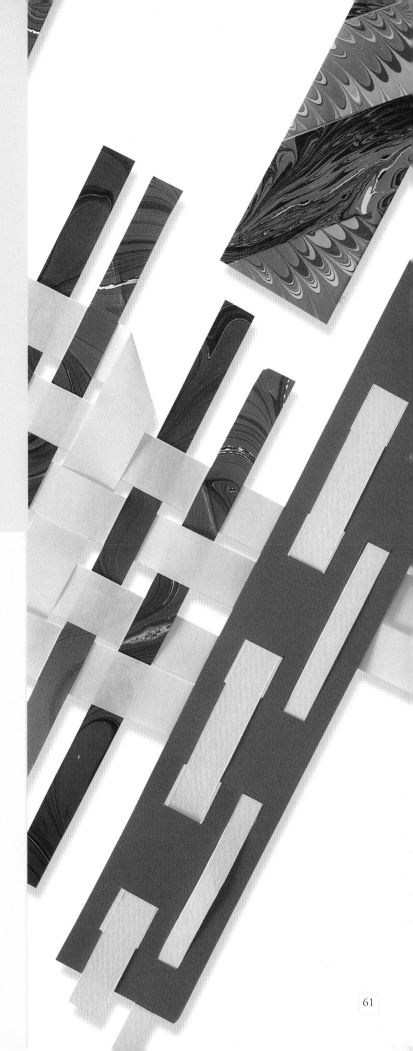

Golden Braid *Choker*

This choker is not only beautiful, but you can make it quickly and with ease. The gold foil

accents the yellow and peach in the tie-dyed paper I found at my local art supply store.

Braid it just as you would braid hair, except you are working with flat, two-dimensional

pieces that need to be folded and creased as you weave them together. To make wearing this

choker more comfortable, it is lined with interfacing that can easily be found in fabric or

craft stores. Follow the illustrations and you will soon be wearing this piece yourself.

Materials

Piece of gold foil paper, 4" × 20"
(10 cm × 51 cm)

Piece of tie-dyed peach paper, 3" × 20"
(8 cm × 51 cm)

1" (3 cm) gold choker clip

PVA glue

Ruler

Scissors

Piece of interfacing, ¾" × 14" (2 cm × 36 cm)

Pliers

Pencil

Fold the gold foil paper in half,
with the glue on the inside.

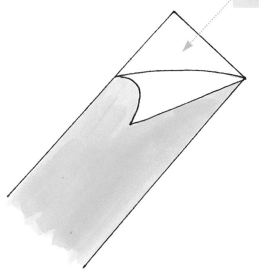

Getting Started

Brush a thin coat of glue on the back side of the gold
paper and fold it in half lengthwise so that the piece
now measures 2" × 20" (5 cm × 51 cm). Firmly press
the two sides together, making sure that there are no
air bubbles. Cut three ½" × 20" (1 cm × 51 cm) strips
from this piece. Cut six ⅜" × 20" (1 cm × 51 cm) strips
from the peach paper.

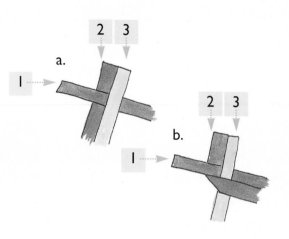

1 Run a thin bead of glue down the middle of one gold strip and lay a peach piece onto the glue, making sure that it is centered. Flip the piece over and glue another peach piece to the other side. Repeat with the remaining gold and peach strips.

2 Lay the three pieces out according to the illustration, and braid them together by folding each strip forward as shown. So that it is easier to understand the illustrations, each strip is represented by a different color even though all three strips are peach. Begin by folding strip number 2 over to the right so that it is parallel to strip number 1.

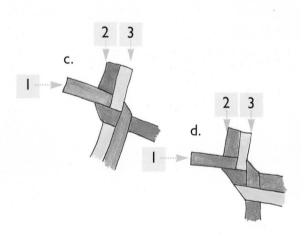

3 Next, fold strip number 1 to the left so that it runs parallel to strip number 3. Then strip number 3 is folded over to run parallel to strip number 2. Continue in this manner for the length of the strips.

4 Apply glue to one side of the braid and center the interfacing onto it.

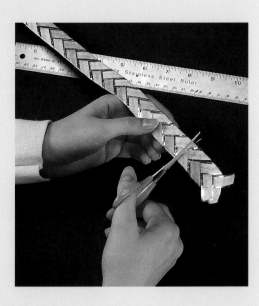

5 Use the scissors to cut off just enough of one end of the braid to have a nice clean and square edge. From that edge, measure off 12" (30 cm) and cut the braid. The choker clasp is adjustable, so the 12" (30 cm) measurement should fit most people.

6 Insert one end of the braid into one side of the choker clip, and use the pliers to bend the clip into place so it grips the paper. Repeat with the other end of the braid and the other side of the clip.

Variation
on a Theme

Colored paper string instead of strips of paper is braided to create this beautiful choker. The quantity of the paper strings used assures the strength and durability for a long-lasting treasure.

Origami Fold
Bracelet

This bold and colorful bracelet is not only decorative but remarkably functional. It is beautiful as a bracelet, yet due to its multiple layers of folds, it is sturdy enough to thread a watch onto and use as a watchband. You can also lengthen the pattern for the bracelet so that it may be used as an anklet or choker, or shorten the strap to decorate the face of a barrette. An entire ensemble of paper jewelry, requiring materials no more common than white paper and tissue paper, could be designed around this easily created strap bracelet.

Materials

Piece of green tissue paper, $1\frac{1}{2}$" × 12"
(4 cm × 30 cm)

Piece of blue tissue paper, $1\frac{1}{2}$" × 12"
(4 cm × 30 cm)

Piece of white copy paper or bond paper,
$1\frac{1}{2}$" × 12" (4 cm × 30 cm)

Full sheet of purple tissue paper

PVA glue

Glue brush

Clipboard

Ruler

Craft knife

Water-based polyurethane

Small paintbrush

2 silver 7 mm jump rings

Silver bracelet clasp

Needle-nosed pliers

Butter knife

Embroidery needle

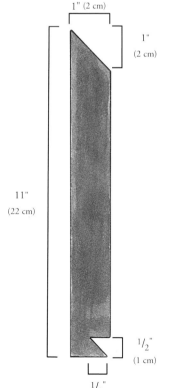

Getting Started

Brush a coat of glue over one side of the white paper
and lay the green tissue paper on top of it. Flip the piece
over and do the same with the blue tissue paper. Follow
the illustrations to cut the paper into the needed shape for
the bracelet. Brush a single coat of polyurethane over each
side of the piece and set it aside to dry for approximately
one hour.

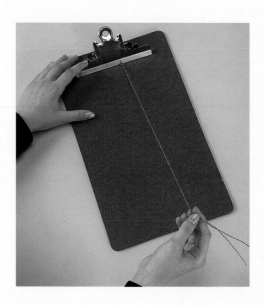

1 From the long side of the purple tissue paper, cut two strips of paper measuring ½" (1 cm) wide, and, starting at one end, twist each tightly so that each forms a thin string.

2 Hold the ends of each string together and slip them under the clip of the clipboard. Twist each string so tightly that it starts to curl back on itself. Then, hold the two free ends of the strings together and twist them in the opposite direction that you originally twisted them. Remove this double string from the clipboard and brush a coat of polyurethane over it. Set it aside to dry.

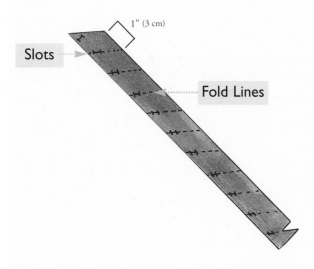

1" (3 cm)

Slots

Fold Lines

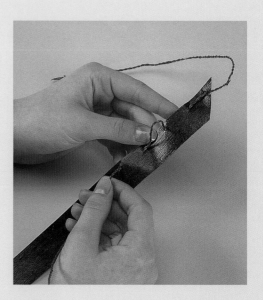

3 Once the green and blue piece is dry, mark off the paper in intervals of 1" (3 cm) as shown. Use the ruler and the butter knife to connect the marks as described earlier. This will crease the fibers so that it will be easier to fold the paper. Finally, use the craft knife to cut the slots in the paper according to the illustration.

4 Hold the piece in front of you, blue side up. Starting at the pointed end, thread the purple string up from the back and down through the next slot in the paper. Continue in this manner for the length of the strip.

5 Place the piece in front of you, blue side up again, and fold along the first bend line so that the green side is now showing. Fold the paper back along the second fold line so that the blue side is showing again. Continue in this manner for the length of the strip. Use a bit of glue to secure all the folds in place.

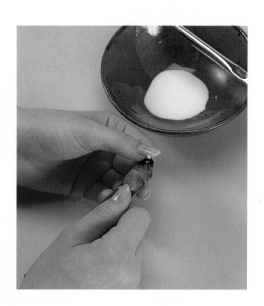

6 Cut the ends of the purple string so that it extends only ¼" (.5 cm) beyond the edge of the strip. On both ends of the paper, fold the blue point back, capturing the end of the purple string in the fold. Glue the ends in place.

7 Use the needle to punch a hole in the point at each end of the bracelet. Thread a jump ring through each hole with the needle-nosed pliers, and then attach the clasp to one of the jump rings.

Variation on a Theme

This strap bracelet, folded exactly the same way as the one in the project, features cutouts that are removed to reveal overlapping colors.

Pinwheel *Earrings*

These pinwheels may appear to be fragile, but they are not too delicate to touch or to wear because they are made of thick, sturdy wallpaper. Wallpaper stores will frequently give away books of samples when a line of paper is discontinued or sold out. Wallpaper designed for the kitchen or bath is vinyl and therefore already water-proofed. This eliminates the need to coat the pinwheels with polyurethane without compromising the durability of the earrings.

Materials

Piece of plaid wallpaper, 9" × 5" (23 cm × 13 cm)

PVA glue

Glue brush

Ruler

Craft knife

4 silver 4 mm jump rings

2 kidney wire earring hooks

2 clothespins

Embroidery needle

Needle-nosed pliers

Getting Started

Cut out two squares of the section of the plaid where the warp and the weft lines intersect and two squares of the white paper from between the plaid strips, each measuring at least 1½" (4 cm) square. Glue a white square and a plaid square back to back. Press down firmly to assure that there are no air bubbles. Repeat with the other two squares.

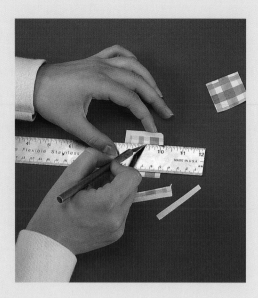

1 Trim each square of wallpaper so that it measures exactly 1½" (4 cm) across. Repeat with the other section of square wallpaper.

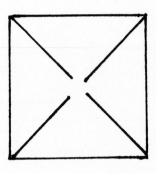

2 Use the ruler and the craft knife to cut each square along the lines shown in the illustration.

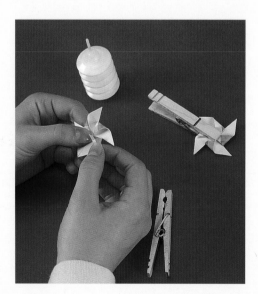

3 The white side of the square will be the inside of the pinwheel. Place a dot of glue in the center of this square, fold a corner into the middle and hold it in place. Continue adding a dot of glue and folding in every other corner until four have been glued in place. Use a clothes-pin to hold the corners in place while the glue dries, about one hour. Repeat with the other square of paper.

4 Once the glue has dried, use the needle to punch a hole in one point of each pinwheel, as shown.

5 With the needle-nosed pliers, thread a jump ring through the hole of one pinwheel, and then link another ring to the first. Repeat with the other pinwheel.

6 To finish off the earrings, simply slip one pinwheel onto each kidney wire earring back.

Variation on a Theme

The pinwheels are a fun form to play with, and you can easily adapt them to a number of earring styles. This pair of earrings puts smaller pinwheels onto post earring backs.

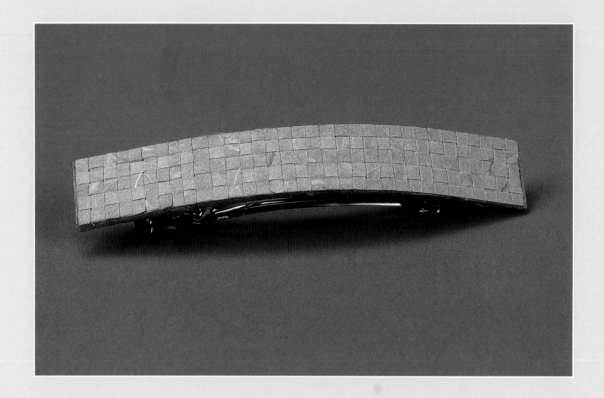

Basket Weave *Barrette*

As school children, many of us made basket weave place mats from various colors of
construction paper. The same method used to make those childhood mats is the basis for
this fashionable barrette. The narrow strips of paper in muted colors give the barrette a
refined look. It is so easy to make, it will seem like child's play, but the result is a mature
personal accessory that will endure for years.

Materials

Barrette clip

Piece of $\frac{1}{16}$" (2 mm) chipboard or cardboard, $\frac{5}{8}$" × 4" (2 cm × 10 cm)

Piece of purple paper, 6 $\frac{1}{2}$" × 5" (17 cm × 13 cm)

Piece of green paper, 6 $\frac{1}{2}$" × 5" (17 cm × 13 cm)

PVA glue

Glue brush

3 clothespins

Clipboard

Ruler

Pencil

Scissors or craft knife

Embroidery needle

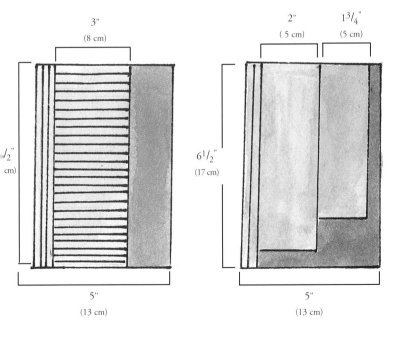

Getting Started

Begin by following the pattern to cut all the pieces of paper required to make this project. From the purple paper you need 3 strips measuring $\frac{1}{8}$" × 6 $\frac{1}{2}$" (.3 cm × 17 cm) and 32 strips measuring $\frac{1}{8}$" × 3" (.3 cm × 8 cm). From the green paper you need two strips measuring $\frac{1}{8}$" × 6 $\frac{1}{2}$" (.3 cm × 17 cm), a 2" × 6" (5 cm × 15 cm) piece, and a 5" × 1 $\frac{3}{4}$" (13 cm × 5 cm) piece. Line up the five long strips of paper side by side, starting with a purple strip and alternating colors. Slip the first $\frac{1}{2}$" (1 cm) of the ends of the paper beneath the clipboard clip.

1 The five long strips will be the warp of your weaving. With all of the short strips for the weft, use the basic basket weave technique described in How to Basket Weave on page 59 to create the decorative woven portion of the barrette. Use the tip of the needle to push the narrow strips close to each other, and be sure to center the weft strips on the warp.

2 Spread a thin coat of glue over one side of the piece of green paper measuring 2" × 6" (5 cm × 15 cm). Carefully remove the woven piece from the clipboard, and, making sure that it stays square, lay it into the glue on top of the green paper. Gently press the woven strips into the glue to assure that there are no air bubbles.

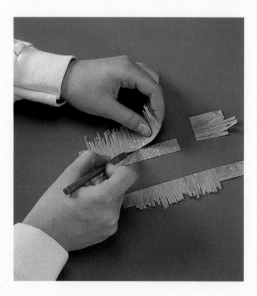

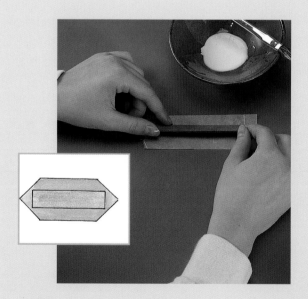

3 You will notice that there is about ¾" (2 cm) of unwoven weft strips on either side of the weaving and a bit of the warp strips overhanging the top and bottom. Using the craft knife, trim the unwoven portion so the piece measures ⅝" × 4" (2 cm × 10 cm). This is the decorative face of the barrette.

4 To make the barrette base, spread a thin coat of glue on one side of the chipboard, and, making sure that it is centered, press it firmly glue side down onto the 5" × 1¾" (13 cm × 5 cm) green paper. Trim the corners of the green paper as shown in the illustration. Leave ⅛" (.3 cm) of paper showing beyond the corner of the board, so the edge will be completely covered.

5 Brush a thin coat of glue onto the exposed paper around the board and fold the two short edges tightly up and over the board. Continue by folding the two longer sides up and over the board in the same fashion, paying special attention to the corners. Use either your fingers or the point of the needle to tuck in the corners as you would when wrapping a present.

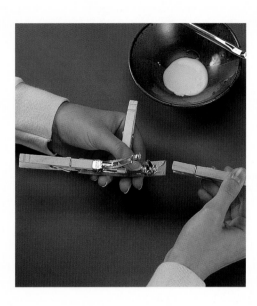

6 Apply a generous coat of PVA glue to the top side of the barrette clip. Center the paper-covered board over the clip and use a clothespin to secure the centers of each to the other. Gently bend the board to the curve of the clip using a clothespin to hold each end in place. Leave the three pins securing the piece while the glue dries, about one hour.

7 Once the glue holding the paper-covered board to the clip has dried, brush a thin coat of PVA over the top of the board and carefully lay the woven piece in place. Press it firmly but gently into the glue, making sure there are no air bubbles.

Variation
on a Theme

Simply changing the shape of the board is an easy way to achieve a whole new look for the barrette. This diamond-shaped barrette also includes twice as many colors as the previous project.

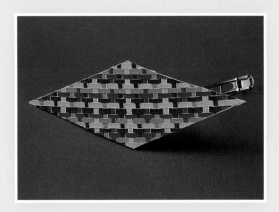

How to Make Paper

*M*aking paper is fun, easy, and rewarding, and requires only a few household items, some scraps of paper, and various art supplies. This recipe produces beautiful navy-colored paper, but you can create a different colored paper simply by substituting the blue dye with another color; or after you have made a few blue sheets of paper, add some yellow or red dye to the pulp to produce either green or purple sheets of paper. For a personal touch, experiment with different paper types, or add objects such as petals or lace to the pulp. Once you discover how quickly you can create beautiful paper, you will find yourself with a growing stack of unique papers to use for countless creative projects.

Materials

Paper scraps

Blender

Water

Blue dye

Large, shallow vat (large enough to contain deckle and mold)

8½" × 11" (22 cm × 28 cm) deckle and mold

2 pieces of felt just larger than the paper you are making

Pressing boards

Sheet of foam core or other smooth surface

Towels and sponges

Bucket

Putty or butter knife

1

Tear the paper into small pieces, measuring no more than 1" (3 cm) square, and place them in the bucket. Add enough water to cover the paper and let it soak overnight to soften the fibers. The next day, put a small handful of the paper pieces into the blender with a little bit of water and blend until the pulp is smooth (it should resemble the consistency of cooked oatmeal). Repeat until all of the soaked paper bits have been made into pulp. Pour into the shallow vat and add several tablespoons of blue dye until you have created a rich, blue mixture.

2

Mix enough water into the pulp so that it has a soupy consistency (the more water you add to the pulp, the thinner the sheet of paper will be). Agitate the mixture to ensure an even dispersion of the pulp. Stack the mold on top of the deckle and, beginning at one side of the vat, slip the deckle and mold beneath the surface of the pulp solution in one smooth movement.

3

Lift the deckle and mold straight up out of the vat and gently shake them to ensure an even dispersion of the paper pulp. Allow as much water as possible to drain off, and remove the mold from the top of the deckle.

4

To prevent the pulp from sticking to the felts, soak them in water and then wring them out. Place one pressing board on the work surface with a piece of felt on top of it. In a quick, smooth motion flip the deckle over onto the felt so that the sheet of paper you are forming is trapped between the screen of the deckle and the felt. With a towel or sponge, press against the screen of the deckle to squeeze out as much water from the pulp sheet as possible. Gently remove the deckle, leaving the pulp sheet on the felt. If the pulp starts to tear as you lift off the deckle, press out more water before continuing.

5

Lay the other felt on top of the pulp sheet and the other pressing board on top of that. Press the sheet firmly between the two boards to remove more water. You may find that standing on the boards is the easiest way to do this. Carefully remove the top board and felt.

6

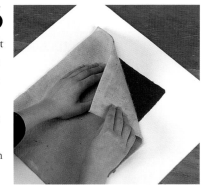

Lift the felt that the sheet of paper is on and turn it over onto the foam core, pulp side down. Press the sheet against the foam core and gently peel the felt away from the sheet of paper. If the paper starts to tear, press it back against the foam to remove more moisture before continuing to peel off the felt. Leave the newly formed sheet of paper on the foam for several hours to dry.

7

When the edges of the paper sheet start to pull away from the foam core, and the center of the sheet feels dry to the touch, slip a putty or butter knife between the paper and the foam core, and gently pry the paper from the surface.

Paper-Making Tips

1 To make your own deckle and mold set, use two matching picture frames and window screening (available at any hardware store) to cover the opening of one frame. Remove the glass, backing, and stands from the frames so that only the front portion of the frame remains. Wrap the screening around one frame and staple or glue it in place. This frame is now the deckle. Stack the other frame on top of the deckle to use it as the mold for your paper.

2 Use cookie cutters as molds on top of a deckle to make small, fun shaped pieces of paper to use for invitations or name tags.

3 Make larger sheets of paper by lining up and slightly overlapping multiple sheets of the unpressed, wet paper on a large pressing board and then press them all at once to form a bigger composite piece of paper.

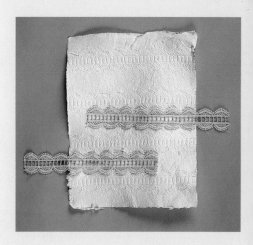

About the Author

Jessica Wrobel is one of the most exciting and innovative designers working today. Wrobel's highly successful studio work is well known for a wide variety of fine art, and features hand-marbled papers and fabrics, custom-designed clothing, jewelry, home accessories, and fresh florals. Wrobel devotes much of her time to teaching community art classes, in expression of her strong belief that art should be shared.

Acknowledgments

With special thanks to Tara, for her lovely hands; Mary McCarthy, whose inspiration led me down this path; and Mom and Dad, for letting me be who I am.

Dedicated to Tom, with love.

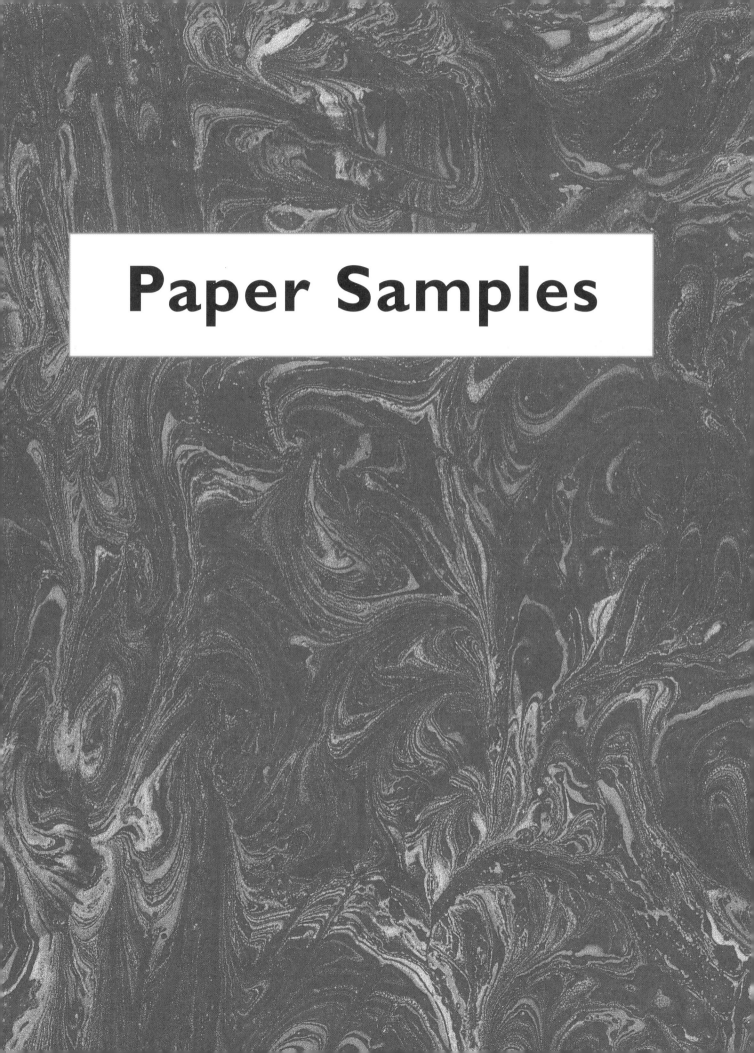

Paper Samples